Northern New Mexico Recipes Volume 1

Edition 2

I0758409

Romero Family

1

Table of Contents

EARLY SETTLERS OF NEW MEXICO

The Pueblo people were the first people to settle in the area that is now known as New Mexico. Around the year 800 CE, they established their homes in what is now known as the Rio Grande Valley. Over the course of the subsequent few centuries, they established large villages and developed a sophisticated culture that included a unique architecture and   pottery.

Around the year 1200 CE, people of the Navajo and Apache tribes first started moving into the area. Eventually, the Navajo people settled in the western part of the state, while the Apache people established their communities in the   eastern   part   of   the   state.

In 1598, a Spanish expedition led by Don Juan de Onate established a settlement at San Juan Pueblo. This marked the beginning of Spanish colonization in New Mexico. The first European settlement in what is now the United States of   America   was   located   here.

In 1610, when Santa Fe was established as the capital of New Mexico, the beginning of the Spanish colonial period got under way in earnest. The Spanish were the ones who introduced Catholicism to the region, and as a result, a significant number of the Pueblo people converted to the religion.

Despite this, the relationships between the Spanish and the Pueblo people were frequently contentious. The Pueblo people rose up against Spanish rule in 1680 and drove the settlers out of Santa Fe as a result of their victory. However, the uprising only lasted for a short period of time, and the Spanish quickly retook control of the region.

Mexico achieved its independence from Spain in the year 1821. Santa Fe was reestablished as the capital after New

4

Mexico was officially incorporated into Mexico. In 1846, there were approximately 6,000 Americans living in the territory of New Mexico, and Mexico had permitted the settlement of New Mexico by Americans. As a result, tensions rose between Mexicans and Americans, which ultimately led to the United States declaring war on Mexico in the year 1846.

As part of the Treaty of Guadalupe Hidalgo, which ended a brief war between the two countries, Mexico handed over New Mexico to the United States. The newly formed American territory chose Santa Fe to serve as its capital.

The year 1912 marked the year that New Mexico became the 47th state to join the Union. Santa Fe continues to serve as the state's capital even today.

The history of New Mexico goes back a very long time and is very rich. The Pueblo people were the first known inhabitants of this area, and they left behind a remarkable legacy of artistic and cultural expression. The state's history as a Spanish colony, its period of incorporation into Mexico, and its current standing as an American state have all contributed to the formation of the state. People from all walks of life can be found living in New Mexico today, which contributes to the state's vibrant culture and rich diversity.

HISTORY OF NORTHERN NEW MEXICAN FOOD

The history of Northern New Mexican cuisine is long and illustrious. The indigenous cuisine of Mesoamerica was combined with European cuisine, particularly Spanish cuisine, that was brought to the Americas during the Spanish colonization of the region. As these settlers made their way to what is now known as North New Mexico they established a unique take on the foods of Central America. The Northern New Mexican cuisine that resulted from the fusion of these two cultures was entirely original.

Over the course of its history, Northern New Mexican cuisine has been shaped by a variety of factors, including the climate and geography of the state as well as its cultural heritage. For instance, the hot and dry climate of Mexico has resulted in the creation of dishes best suited for farms and ranches of the area. The geography of the state also played a part in the development of its cuisine. New Mexico is home to a diverse range of ecosystems, each of which is characterized by its own unique flora and fauna. This diversity has led to the incorporation of a wide range of distinct flavors and textures into Northern New Mexican cuisine.

As a result of New Mexico's long history of cultural exchange, the state developed a culinary tradition that is completely distinct. The arrival of Spanish colonists in the area had a significant impact on the indigenous cultures of the region. In turn, the foods and methods of cooking that were common among the indigenous peoples of Northern New Mexico had a significant impact on the development of Spanish cuisine. The end result is a cuisine that is in every heart of the land and the people who have lived there.

SALSA

Salsa Ingredients:

1 can (15 oz) diced tomatoes, undrained
1/4 of a cup of minced onion
4 oz finely chopped red bell pepper
1 jalapeno, seeded and chopped very finely
8 oz of diced green chile
1 garlic clove, finely chopped
1/2 tsp salt
1/4 tsp sugar
2 tsp of ground cumin
1/4 tsp black pepper
1/4 cup of fresh cilantro leaves, chopped

Salsa Instructions:

1. Put all of the ingredients, besides the cilantro, into a medium pot and mix well.

2. Turn the heat on to a low medium heat. Bring the salsa to a low simmer. Stir often to ensure none of the ingredients stick to the bottom of the pan. This should take about 5 – 10 minutes.

3. Remove the pot from the stove and allow the salsa to cool.

4. Cover and place in the refrigerator if not eaten right away. Salsa can be served warm or cold depending on your preference.

5. Serve with chips, on tacos, or as a condiment for various dishes.

GUACAMOLE

Guacamole Ingredients:

4 ripe avocados, diced

1/2 red onion, diced

1 large jalapeno, diced

2 cloves garlic, minced

1/4 cup cilantro, chopped

juice of 1 lime

salt and pepper, to taste

Optional Ingredients:

1 medium tomato diced

4 oz of green chile

Guacamole Instructions:

- Place the avocado, red onion, jalapeno, garlic, and cilantro in a bowl of a medium size and mix well.

- Season to taste with salt and pepper, and then add lime juice.

- Serve with chips or incorporate as a topping for various dishes

SALSA VERDE

Ingredients:

1 lb. tomatillos, husks removed
1/2 medium white onion diced
2 cloves garlic, minced
1 jalapeño pepper diced
1/4 cup chopped cilantro
1 tbsp. lime juice
Salt and pepper to taste

Salsa Verde Instructions:

1. Preheat the oven temperature to 375 degrees Fahrenheit.

2. Arrange the tomatillos, onion, garlic, and jalapeno peppers in a single layer on a baking sheet. Roast everything for fifteen to twenty minutes, stirring once or twice, until it is all soft and has a slightly charred appearance around the edges.

3. After the mixture has had some time to slightly cool, transfer it to a blender or food processor and add the cilantro as well as the lime juice. After seasoning with salt and pepper, blend the mixture until it is completely smooth.

4. Serve with chips or utilize as a condiment for tacos or meats that have been grilled. Enjoy!

RED ENCHILADA SAUCE

Ingredients:

2 tablespoons vegetable oil

6 cloves garlic, minced

1 onion, diced

2 tablespoon chili powder

1 teaspoon cumin

1 teaspoon smoked paprika

1/2 teaspoon oregano

2 cups chicken or beef broth

1 (15-ounce) can tomato sauce

1 (14.5-ounce) can diced tomatoes, undrained

3 tablespoons chopped fresh cilantro leaves

Red Enchilada Sauce Instructions:

Warm the oil in a large saucepan by placing it over a heat source of medium intensity. Put in the minced garlic, chopped onion, chili powder, cumin, smoked paprika, oregano, cilantro, and a pinch of each of the seasonings listed above. Cook for about 5 minutes, or until the vegetables have reached the desired degree of tenderness.

The broth, tomato sauce, and diced tomatoes should all be added now. Bring to a simmer and continue cooking for approximately twenty minutes, or until the sauce has thickened. After the sauce has had time to cool, transfer it to a blender and process it until you have a sauce that is thick but not chunky.

FLOUR TORTILLAS

Ingredients:

2 cup all-purpose flour

1 teaspoon salt

2 tablespoon lard or vegetable shortening

4 tablespoons cold water

Flour tortillas Instructions:

1. Put the flour and salt into a large bowl and mix them together. Slowly mix in the lard or shortening you're using until it looks like coarse crumbs. Add the cold water gradually while stirring the mixture constantly until it forms a ball.

2. On a surface that has been lightly floured, roll out the dough to a desired thickness

3. Preheat griddle or skillet over medium heat. Heat tortillas for one to two minutes on each side, or until they have golden brown spots that start to appear.

CORN TORTILLAS

Ingredients:

2 cups of masa harina

1 1/2 cups of warm water

1/2 teaspoon of salt

Corn Tortillas Instructions:

1. Place the masa harina and salt in a large bowl and mix well with your hands. After adding the warm water, stir the ingredients together until they come together to form a dough.

2. Give the dough a few minutes of kneading, then wrap it in a damp towel and set it aside for a period of thirty minutes to rest.

3. Bring a pan up to a medium temperature.

4. Form the dough into 10 dough balls. Make a flat disc out of each ball of dough by pressing it down with your hands or a rolling pin.

5. Place the tortillas on the pan and cook them for one to two minutes on each side, or until they have a light browning on both sides and are fully cooked.

BIRRIA TACOS

Ingredients:

2 lbs. of boneless beef chuck roast

1 onion, diced

3 cloves of garlic, minced

2 tablespoons of chili powder

2 teaspoon of cumin

1 teaspoon of oregano

1/2 teaspoon of salt

1/2 teaspoon of black pepper

2 cups of beef broth

2 tablespoons of tomato paste

12 corn tortillas

1 1/2 cup of shredded cheese

1/2 cup of chopped cilantro

2 tablespoons of vegetable oil

3 cups enchilada sauce or pozole broth

Birria Tacos Instructions:

1. Preheat a large pot over medium heat. Brown the goat (or beef) roast on all sides in the pot or oven.

2. Put in the chopped onion and garlic, along with the chili powder, cumin, oregano, salt, and black pepper. Stir to combine.

3. Add the tomato paste and the beef broth to the pan. The mixture should be heated to a low simmer.

4. Place a lid on the pot and cook the beef over low heat until it can be easily pierced with a fork, which should take about three hours.

5. Take the beef out of the pot and, using two forks, shred it.

6. Place the vegetable oil and 2 tspn of the enchilada sauce or pozole broth in a pan and heat to a medium high heat

7. Fill a tortilla one at a time with the shredded roast and cheese in a folded shell shape. And place in the pan. Cook on both sides lightly crisping up the shell and melting the cheese.

8. Serve everyone 1 cup of warmed enchilada sauce or pozole broth on the side to dip their tacos in as they eat.

FISH TACOS

Ingredients:

1 lb. fish (tilapia, mahi-mahi, or catfish)

8–10 small soft tacos

2 tablespoons olive oil

1 tablespoon lime juice

1 teaspoon chili powder

1 teaspoon cumin

sea salt and freshly ground black pepper to taste

For the Taco slaw:

1 cup shredded cabbage (red or green)

2 tablespoons chopped fresh cilantro leaves

1 tablespoon diced red onion

1 tablespoon olive oil

1 tablespoon lime juice

Fish Tacos Instructions:

1. Preheat oven to 350 degrees.

2. In a small bowl, combine the chili powder, cumin, salt, and pepper along with the lime juice, olive oil, and lime juice. Coat the fish with the above ingredients.

3. Arrange the fish in a single layer on a baking sheet and bake it for about ten minutes, or until it is fully cooked.

4. In the meantime, prepare the slaw by combining in a large bowl the cabbage, cilantro, red onion, olive oil, and lime juice.

5. To assemble the tacos, place a piece of cooked fish in the middle of each taco shell and then add a layer of slaw on top of the fish. Immediately serve after cooking.

CARNE ASADA TACOS

Ingredients:

1 lb flank steak

2 tablespoon vegetable oil

1/4 cup water

2 cloves garlic, minced

3 teaspoons chili powder

2 teaspoons cumin

1 teaspoon salt

1/2 teaspoon black pepper

9 corn tortillas

1 cup salsa

1/2 cup sour cream

1 avocado, diced

1 tomato, diced

1/4 cup chopped cilantro

Carne Asada Instructions:

1. Put the vegetable oil, garlic, chili powder, cumin, salt, and pepper into a small bowl and mix them together. Place the steak in a zip-lock bag with the marinade and put in the refrigerator for at least an hour before cooking.

2. Bring a pan or grill up to a medium-high heat

3. Place the steak on the grill and cook it for 5-7 minutes per side, or until it reaches your preference. Take the meat off the grill, and after letting it rest for five minutes, slice it into thin strips.

4. Assemble the tacos by placing a few strips of steak in the bottom of each taco shell and then topping them with salsa, sour cream, avocado, tomato, and cilantro.

CARNITAS

Ingredients:

1 lb pork shoulder

1 medium onion, diced

4 cloves garlic, minced

1 orange, juiced

1 lime, juiced

3 teaspoons chili powder

1 teaspoon cumin

1 teaspoon smoked paprika

3 tablespoons vegetable oil

Carnitas Instructions:

Prepare the oven by heating it to 375 degrees. Put the pork shoulder, onion, garlic, citrus juices (orange and lime), chili powder, cumin, smoked paprika, and vegetable oil in a large bowl or a zip-lock bag and mix well. Combine everything by thoroughly mixing it.

Roast the mixture in the oven for 45 minutes to 1 hour, or until the pork is fully cooked, after spreading it out in a single layer on a baking sheet.

Take out of the oven and allow to slightly cool before shredding with a fork or chopping into small pieces.

BARBACOA

Ingredients:

1 lb. beef chuck roast

1 medium onion, chopped

3 cloves garlic, minced

1 chipotle pepper in adobo sauce, minced

3 tbsp. chili powder

2 tsp. cumin

1 tsp. oregano

3/4 cup beef broth or water

Salt and pepper to taste

Barbacoa Instructions:

1) Preheat oven to 375 degrees F.

2) Brown the beef on all sides in a large pot over high heat. After a few minutes of sauteing, add the onions, garlic, and chipotle pepper, and cook until the onion mixture becomes fragrant. Mix in the chili powder, cumin, and oregano until evenly distributed. The beef broth or water should be added, and then the dish should be seasoned with salt and pepper.

3) Once the mixture has reached a simmer, cover it and place it in the oven. Bake for about two to three hours, or until the beef is very tender.

4) Take the beef out of the oven and use a fork to shred it. Include tortillas in the serving.

CARNE ADOVADA

Ingredients:

2 lbs. of pork shoulder, trimmed and cut into 1-inch cubes

1 large onion, chopped

3 cloves of garlic, minced

3 tablespoons of chili powder

1 tablespoon of cumin

1 teaspoon of oregano

1/2 teaspoon of salt

1/2 teaspoon of black pepper

1 (14.5 oz) can of diced tomatoes, undrained

Carne Adovada Instructions:

1. In a large pot over medium heat, combine the pork cubes, onion, garlic, chili powder, cumin, oregano, salt, and black pepper cook for 3 – 5 minutes

2. Stir in the diced tomatoes and bring to a simmer.

3. Reduce heat to low and cover.

4. Simmer on stove for 1 to 1 1/2 hours and the pork is fully cooked and tender.

5. Serve with warm flour tortillas

STACKED ENCHILADAS

While most people are familiar with the typical rolled enchiladas found in most Mexican Restaurants. Stacked Enchiladas are a New Mexico dish. The recipe is listed below.

Ingredients:

1 lb ground beef

1/2 medium onion, diced

2 cups red enchilada sauce

1 can (15 oz) pinto beans, rinsed and drained

10 corn tortillas

2 cups shredded cheese

2 tbsp of vegetable oil

Sour cream (optional)

2 diced black olives

Stacked Enchiladas Instructions:

1. Preheat the oven to 350 degrees

2. In a large skillet, cook the ground beef and the onion over medium-high heat until the beef is browned.

3. Drain the fat from the ground beef and set the beef aside

4. Warm the enchilada sauce in a small pot. Stir frequently.

5. in the skillet you cooked the ground beef add 2 tbsp of vegetable oil and warm over a medium high heat.

6. When the oil is hot place one corn tortilla at a time in the oil. Heat each side of the corn tortilla for 5-10 seconds.

7. Place each cooked tortilla on a plate lined with a paper towel to catch any dripping oil from the cooked cooked corn tortillas

8a. If you have plates that are oven safe proceed with this step. Spread a small amount of enchilada sauce on the plate. Place one corn tortilla on the sauce. Place a layer of ground beef and a layer of cheese. Make two layers of the stacked enchiladas. At the top of the stack should be a corn tortilla smothered with enchilada sauce and a final layer of shredded cheese. Place oven safe plate in the preheated oven until the cheese has melted.

8b. If you do not have oven safe plates proceed with this step. Place a small amount of enchilada sauce on the center of the plate. Place a corn tortilla on the sauce. Place a layer of ground beef and a layer of cheese. Make two layers of stacked enchiladas. At the top of the stack should be a corn tortilla smothered with enchilada sauce and a final layer of shredded cheese. Place this plate in a microwave and warm until cheese has melted

9. Take the plate out of the oven or microwave utilizing a pot holder.

10. If desired, serve with sour cream, lettuce, diced tomato, olives, and chopped green onions on top of the dish and serve.

GREEN CHILE CHICKEN ENCHILADAS

Ingredients:

2 tablespoons vegetable oil

1 onion, diced

3 cloves garlic, minced

2 pounds boneless, skinless chicken breasts, cut into bite-sized pieces

Salt and pepper to taste

2 tablespoons all-purpose flour

1 tablespoon chili powder

1 teaspoon cumin

3 cups green chile enchilada sauce

9 corn tortillas

Optional toppings: shredded cheese, sour cream, chopped green onions, diced avocado

Green Chile Chicken Enchiladas Instructions:

1. Prepare the oven by preheating it to 375 degrees F. (190 degrees.

2. To preheat the olive oil, place it in a large skillet and set it over medium-high heat. Once the onion and garlic have softened, which should take about 5 minutes, add them to the pan. To the pan, add the pieces of chicken, and season with salt and pepper. Continue cooking for about 5 minutes more, or until the meat is browned.

3. To the pan, add the flour, chili powder, and cumin, and stir to combine the ingredients. After adding the green enchilada sauce, continue to cook the mixture until it begins to bubble. Take the dish away from the heat.

4. To assemble enchiladas, fill the middle of each tortilla with two tablespoons of the chicken mixture and roll up the tortilla. Roll up tightly and then place in a baking dish with the seam side down.

5. The tortillas should be rolled tightly before the remaining enchilada sauce is added on top. If you'd like, you can top it with some shredded cheese.

35

6. Bake in an oven that has been preheated until the cheese is melted and bubbling, which should take about ten minutes. Serve right away, topping each portion with avocado, sour cream, and green onions

SPANISH RICE

Ingredients:

1 cup long grain white rice

2 cups chicken broth

1 tablespoon olive oil

1 small onion, diced

1 red bell pepper, diced

1 green bell pepper, diced

4 cloves garlic, minced

1 teaspoon chili powder

1 teaspoon cumin powder

Salt and pepper, to taste

Spanish Rice Instructions:

1. Place the chicken broth in a large saucepan and bring it up to a boil.
2. Include the rice in the mixture, and give it a good stir.
3. Cover the pan, lower the heat to low, and let the mixture simmer for twenty minutes.
4. While that is going on, bring the oil to a simmer in a large skillet set over medium heat.
5. Stir in the garlic, chili powder, and cumin powder along with the onion and bell peppers.
6. Continue to cook, stirring the vegetables occasionally, until they are fork-tender.
7. Add the rice that has been cooked and mix everything together.
8. Add salt and pepper to taste, according to your preference.

FRITO PIE

Ingredients:

15 oz can of Pinto Beans drained and rinsed

1 tsp of chili powder

1/2 cup salsa

1 cup shredded cheese

1 package (10 oz) fritos

Frito Pie Instructions:

1. Preheat oven to 350 degrees.

2. In a medium bowl, mix together black beans, chili powder, salsa, and cheese.

3. Spread the mixture over the fritos.

4. Bake for 10-15 minutes, or until the cheese is melted and bubbly.

BEANS AND RED CHILE

Ingredients:

1 lb dry pinto beans

4 cups water

1 large white onion, diced

3 cloves garlic, minced

3 tablespoons chili powder

2 teaspoons cumin

1 teaspoon oregano

salt and pepper to taste

1 (15-ounce) can diced tomatoes, undrained

1 (4-ounce can diced green chiles, undrained)

2 tablespoons chopped fresh cilantro leaves

Beans and Red Chile Instructions:

1. Sort through beans for any foreign objects. Discard foreign objects leaving only the beans.

2. Soak the beans overnight in 4 cups of water. Drain and rinse the beans.

3. In a large pot, combine the beans, 4 cups of water, onion, garlic, chili powder, cumin, oregano and salt. Bring to a boil over medium heat.

4. Reduce the heat to low and simmer for 2 to 3 hours, or until the beans are tender. Add the tomatoes, green chiles and cilantro and simmer for another 15 minutes.

SOPAPILLAS

Ingredients:

1lb all purpose flour

2 tsp. baking powder

1/2 tsp. salt

3 tbsp. sugar

1/4 cup shortening or lard, melted

1 cup warm water

Vegetable oil, for frying

Sopapillas Instructions:

Flour, baking powder, salt, and sugar should all be mixed together in a large bowl. After adding the melted shortening or lard and stirring in the warm water, make sure everything is thoroughly combined.

Knead the dough for about five minutes after turning it out onto a floured surface. Put the dough in a bowl that has been greased, cover it, and set it aside in a warm place to rise for about an hour.

Prepare a large griddle or skillet by heating it over medium-high heat and adding sufficient vegetable oil to cover the base of the cooking surface.

The dough should be divided into 12 pieces, and each piece should be flattened with a rolling pin. Do not flatten to thin as the pieces will need to be thick enough to bubble up and rise when cooked. Place in the hot oil cooking both sides. Fry the sopapilla until it is golden brown on both sides and has bubbled up.

Place on cooling rack

Serve as a side for dishes or as a sweet treat with honey or confectioner sugar

MOLE

Ingredients:

4 cups water

1 cup Red Chili powder

2 tspn unsweetened chocolate

1 tspn Cumin

½ cup all purpose Flour

2 tbsp garlic powder

1 tspn caldo de pollo

1 tspn creamy Peanut butter

1 tspn onion powder

2 tbsp of raisins

Salt and Pepper to taste

Mole Instructions:

Put the chili powder, flour, cumin, raisins, onion powder, and garlic in a bowl and thoroughly combine the ingredients until there are no more lumps.

It is possible that additional water will be required in order to achieve a smooth and even consistency after the addition of three cups of water and caldo de pollo and stir till mole is thoroughly mixed.

Pour the mole into a preheated medium pot warmed to a medium heat. Add peanut butter and chocolate. Mix thoroughly. Cook for 10-15 minutes stirring periodically.

GREEN CHILE STEW

Ingredients:

4 cups diced green chile

3lbs pork roast

30 oz diced tomatoes

3 tspn cumin

1 med. onion, large chopped

3 cloves garlic minced

3 med potatoes

salt and pepper to taste

1 qt of chicken broth

Green chile stew instructions:

In a preheated medium pot warm the vegetable oil. Add
the 3 lbs of pork roast diced into cubes. Slightly sear pork
on all sides. Add the diced onion and cook till onion is
translucent.

Add garlic, green chile, diced tomatoes, chicken broth ad
potatoes to the pot.

Reduce heat to medium and cook for an hour. Randomly
stir put to prevent anything from sticking to the bottom of
pan.

Serve in a bowl by itself or over eggs.

CHILAQUILAS

Ingredients:

8 chiles guajillo, seeds removed

3 chiles de arbol, seeds removed

3 cloves garlic minced

2 tsp cumin seeds

4 tomatillos

1/4 tsp dried Mexican oregano

2 cups chicken broth

2 tbsp vegetable oil

1 tbsp cilantro

Chilaquiles:

14 Corn Tortillas, each cut into strips

1/2 cup diced white onion

5 eggs, fried

1 avocado sliced

1/4 cup chopped fresh cilantro

1/2 cup queso oaxaca

1/2 cup sour cream

Vegetable oil

Chilaquilas instructions:

Roja Sauce

In a medium saucepan, bring 4 cups of water to a rolling boil. Add chiles quajillo and chiles de arbol. Turn the temperature down to medium. Cook for ten to twelve minutes, or until it has become softer and more tender. Mix in the chopped tomatillos. To remove the bright green color of the tomatillos, continue cooking them for three to five minutes. Tomatillos and chilies should be removed from the water.

Put the chilies and tomatillos that have been cooked, along with the garlic, cumin, and oregano, in a blender. Blend together with one cup of broth until completely smooth, then set aside.

Prepare the oil by heating it in a medium saucepan over medium heat. Mix in the mixture that has been blended, then bring to a boil. Turn the temperature down to medium-low. Stir in epazote or cilantro. Continue to cook for 15 to 20 minutes, or until the sauce has become slightly thicker and the flavors have merged.

Chilaquilas

A high-sided skillet that is two inches deep with oil should be heated over medium heat until the oil begins to boil. Put tortilla wedges in the hot oil one at a time, working in batches, until the tortillas are completely submerged. Fry for two to three minutes, or until all sides have achieved a golden brown color. Place on a baking sheet lined with parchment paper, and allow to cool.

Bring the sauce back up to a low simmer. Take the pan off the heat. Chips should be gently mixed with sauce until they are evenly coated with sauce and have absorbed the majority of the sauce. Divide between the six plates. Put two fried eggs on top of each one. Add some avocado, sour cream, onion, cilantro, and cheese as toppings for the dish.

ESPANOLA MEXICAN PIZZA

Ingredients:

6 Flour Tortillas

1 jalapeno pepper diced

1 serrano pepper diced

1/2 red bell pepper

4 cherry tomatoes

1/4 onion, cut in wedges

10 oz. cooked crumbled chorizo sausage,

1 1/2 cups shredded Oaxaca cheese

2 sliced radishes

3 black olives diced

2 tbsp cilantro

Espanola Mexican Pizza instructions:

53

Turn the broiler on to high. Arrange tomatoes, peppers, onions, and jalapenos in a single layer on a baking sheet lined with aluminum foil. Broil the vegetables for four to six minutes, or until they are charred and tender. Move to a blender and puree until completely smooth. Salt to taste.

Bring the temperature in the oven up to 400 degrees. Arrange the tortillas in a single layer on a large baking sheet that has been lined with parchment paper. Spread a heaping tablespoonful of sauce across each tortilla, leaving a border all the way around the edge. On top, crumble some cheese and sprinkle on some chorizo. Bake the pizza for 10 minutes until cheese has melted and the tortilla has crisped to a golden color.

Garnish with radishes, olives, and cilantro and serve

SHRIMP CEVICHE TOSTADAS

Ingredients:

10 Tostadas

1 pound cooked and peeled medium shrimp

1 large avocado diced

3/4 cup lime juice

1/2 cup lemon juice

1 large tomato diced

2 garlic cloves, minced

1/2 red onion, diced

1 jalapeno pepper diced

2 serrano peppers, sliced

1/2 cup finely chopped cilantro

Salt and pepper to taste

Shrimp Ceviche Tostadas:

55

Mix the onion, garlic, lime juice, lemon juice, peppers, and salt together in a bowl of medium size. Toss the shrimp in the coating and set aside. Cover and refrigerate for 30 minutes. Combine the shrimp, tomato, avocado, and cilantro in a mixing bowl. Spread the mixture on the tostadas and serve.

PRICKLY PEAR CACTUS TOSTADAS

Ingredients:

8 Tostadas

3 cups chopped nopal (prickly-pear) cactus

3 tbsp lime juice

1 cup chopped onion

1/2 cup diced radishes

1 cup diced tomato

1/2 cup cilantro

½ cup oaxaca cheese

1 tbsp olive oil

3/4 cup refried beans

Salt and pepper to taste

Prickly Pear Cactus Tostadas Instructions:

Put the cactus, green chile, onion, tomato, radish, cilantro, lime juice, olive oil, and salt into a bowl and mix them all together. Combine in great detail.

Using the tostada shells, spread refried beans on each of the tostada shells. Cover with the cactus mixture, and oaxaca cheese.

BUNUELOS

Ingredients:

8 Flour Tortillas

4 tsp of cinnamon

2 cups of granulated sugar

3 cups of vegetable oil

Bunuelos Instructions:

Combine the sugar and cinnamon in a large bowl using a whisk to avoid any lumps. Set aside. In a frying pan with a depth of at least 3 inches, bring 1.5 inches of vegetable oil to 325 degrees Fahrenheit using medium-high heat.

Put one tortilla at a time, using the tongs, into the oil that's already been heated. Allow it to get bubbly and crispy before serving. To achieve a golden brown color, turn the coin over. Remove the tortilla from the oil using a slotted spoon, and place it on a plate that has been covered with a paper towel so that any excess oil can drain off. Proceed in the same manner with the remaining tortillas.

Combine the sugar and cinnamon in a bowl of medium size. Take each tortilla that has been cooked and dip it into the mixture.

POBLLADO

Ingredients:

8 Flour Tortillas

1 cup oaxaca cheese

3 poblano chiles, diced

1 cup bread crumbs

2 eggs

4 green onions; sliced

1 cup vegetable oil

Pobllado Instructions:

1. Spoon some chile, cheese, and green onion on top of each flour tortilla.

2. Roll each tortilla up, then use a toothpick to hold it in place. Use a fork to beat the eggs, and then dip the rolls in the egg, followed by the bread crumbs. Fry in oil until golden brown, then drain on paper towels to remove excess oil.

Serve with Sides of salsa and guacamole for dipping

REFRIED BEANS

Ingredients:

5 Tbsp. lard - or vegetable oil

1 1/2 cups of water

1 lb. pinto beans - cooked

1/2 tsp. cumin

1/4 tsp. ground cayenne pepper

1/4 cup of cotija cheese

1/4 cup diced green onion

Refried Beans Instructions:

To preheat the lard, place it in a large skillet and set the heat to medium-high. After adding the beans, give everything a good stir, then cover the pot and let it simmer for 5 minutes.

Start mashing the beans with a wooden spoon. This will cause the beans to have a thickened pulp. Add water as needed while cooking. Simply replace the lid on the pot, wait a few minutes, and mash the beans a little more.

Continue to cook and repeat the mashing of beans and adding water if necessary or until it reaches the desired consistency. In the event that you inadvertently add more water than necessary, simply remove the lid and allow the excess liquid to evaporate in the steam. Mix in the salt, cayenne pepper, cumin, until evenly distributed.

To serve, bring to a warm temperature and top with cotija cheese and green onions

MOLLETES

Ingredients:

4 bolillo rolls, sliced in half

4 tablespoons butter, room temperature

16 oz refried beans

1 cup oaxaca cheese

1/2 small tomato diced

2 jalapenos diced

1/2 medium white onion diced

Molletes Instructions:

Set the temperature in the oven to 400 degrees. Prepare a baking sheet by lining it with parchment paper.

It is necessary to remove some of the bread from the middle of each half of the bolillo halves in order to make room for toppings. On each half, place a light layer of butter.

On each of the buttered halves of the bolillo, spread some warm refried beans. On top of the beans, sprinkling some oaxaca cheese. Put the bolillo halves on the baking sheet that has been prepared.

Cook in an oven that has been preheated until the cheese is melted and bubbling and the bread has become crisp. This should take about 15 minutes.

To make pico de gallo, dice the jalapeno, onion, and tomatoes into small pieces. Sprinkle the pico de gallo over the molletes and serve

9 798844 088155